Bargello

by the

Block

by

Joan Sjuts Waldman

Animas
Quilts
Publishing

600 Main Ave.
Durango, CO 81301
(970) 247-2582

Bargello by the Block

Animas Quilts Publishing
600 Main Ave.
Durango, CO. 81301
(970) 247-2582

ISBN: 1-885156-16-2

Printed on Recycled Paper

Meet Joan Waldman

Joan grew up on a farm near Humphrey, Nebraska. She became interested in quilts about thirty years ago. This interest grew and she began teaching quilt making in the mid-1970s. She is co-founder of the Calico Quilt Club of Columbus, Ne., where she is constantly being blamed for infecting her friends with incurable "quiltitis". Joan is also a member of the Country Piecemakers Quilt Guild of Norfolk, Ne, Nebraska State Quilt Guild, N.Q.A., and A.Q.S.

Acknowledgements

A big thank you goes to my husband, Harold, who so patiently supports me in everything I attempt to do. Also to my good friends Jean Younkin, Shirley Hassler, and Vivian and Gloria Miller for all their valuable suggestions and support while I worked on this book. Thanks also to my grown children Cynthia, Randall and Erick who, during their growing up years, put up with a mother with a needle in her hand.

CREDITS:

Editor	Kim Gjere
Graphics	Jackie Robinson
Photography	Christopher Marona

Introduction

My fascination for strip work was sparked when I purchased the book Weaver Fever by Jackie Robinson. Graph paper and pen put me on the road to exploring the use of the strip set technique to design quilts. Give these quilts a try and then go a step further and design a quilt of your own. Happy stitching.

The Quilts

Cover Photographs:

Front: **Lights 'N Lanterns,** 47" x 57"

Back: **The Wave,** 50" x 60"

General Directions

Sewing Machine

Start with a clean, oiled sewing machine. Use a new needle (size 80/12) and set the stitch length to approximately twelve stitches per inch. Choose one thread color that will blend with all the fabric in the quilt and fill at least five bobbins. A light, medium or dark gray thread works well on most fabrics. Use a neutral or ecru thread on pastel fabrics.

An accurate 1/4" seam is a must for these quilts. An easy seam guide can be made using molefoam (the material used to pad sore feet). Cut a piece of molefoam 1/2" x 1-1/2". Peel the paper backing and place the molefoam on the throat plate of the sewing machine, 1/4" from the needle. To position this correctly, lower the sewing machine needle directly on the 1/4" line of a flat ruler. If the pressure foot extends 1/4" from the needle and the feed dogs will not be interfered with, stick the molefoam directly next to the pressure foot. If the feed dogs will be covered, or the pressure foot is wider than 1/4", place the molefoam in front of the feed dogs and pressure foot.

When sewing the strips, the fabric will slide next to the molefoam and guide the strips to an accurate 1/4" seam. Stitch some practice seams on scraps to check your seam guide.

Fabric

These quilts are sized to fit the newer, thicker mattresses, with at least a 15" drop on each side.

The yardage and directions in this book are based on 44" wide, 100% cotton fabric. Purchase the best fabrics you can afford. Prewashing and drying fabrics is a personal choice. I prewash and dry so that all fabrics are uniformly preshrunk and any fabrics with a bleeding or wrinkling problem are found before they are stitched into the quilt. Press fabrics after washing.

Try metallic lame' to add a sparkle to your quilt. This fabric needs special handling, but is worth it. It must be stabilized or it will stretch out of shape. Use a fusible woven interfacing or a lining of cotton. Interfacing is applied to the lame' before cutting strips. Cotton lining is cut into strips and layered with the lame' before sewing. Metallic fabric is heat sensitive, so use a pressing cloth and less heat to press it.

Fabric requirements are given with each design. An additional 10% has been added to the actual to allow for shrinkage and "small" cutting mistakes. I usually buy an extra 1/4 yard of each fabric. Yardage for borders is based on straight corners; mitered corners require more fabric. Backing yardage has 3% added for shrinkage.

Cutting

The quilts in this book are based on strips cut across 44" fabrics. Cuts are made from selvage to selvage, using a rotary cutter, ruler and mat. Fold the fabric in fourths. The first fold is selvage to selvage. Be sure the fold is flat. If there are wrinkles at the fold line, slide the selvages right or left until the fold lays perfectly flat. Fold again, bringing the folded edge to the selvages. Again, be sure there are no wrinkles and that the first fold and the selvages are even. If folds are not flat you will not get straight strips.

Cut the raw edge off one end of the fabric.

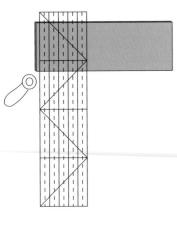

Cut all the strips needed as indicated in the cutting chart. Label each strip, for example: 2-1/2" Fabric A, 2-1/2" Fabric B, etc.

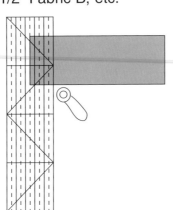

Strip Sets

These quilts are made with blocks which are pieced with rows made from strips sets. A strip set is several strips of fabric sewn together along the long raw edges.

The strips sets are then sliced into rows. The cutting chart indicates the number of strip sets needed for each row. At times you will only need to make 1/4 or 1/2 of a strip set. For a half strip set, cut the strips the width of the fabric, then cut in half to get two 21"-22" strips. For a quarter strip set, cut full strips into fourths, for 10"-11" strips.

Two or more of the rows may be the same strip set in some of the blocks. This is indicated with the strips set drawings. For example: If you are making a block in which rows 2 & 10 are the same and the cutting chart indicates one strip set per row, sew two of this strip set, one for row 2 and one for row 10.

Sorting the Strips

Each quilt has diagrams for the strip set rows. To organize the strips for sewing arrange as follows. Refer to the Row 1 diagram and pick up the first strip listed. Pick up the second strip listed and put it behind the first strip. Place the third strip behind the second. Continue to follow the diagram until all the strips for Row 1 are in your hand.

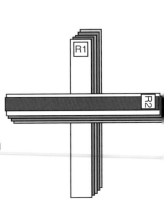

Lay the pile of strips on a table and label them Row 1.

Continue to pick up strips according to the row diagrams. Label each pile of strips with the row number and lay them in crossed piles.

When the final row is pulled, all of the strips that were cut should be used. If not, recheck to see that the rows have the right fabrics and sizes in them.

Stitching

Sew the strip sets using anti-directional stitching. Alternate the direction of stitching with each strip added. The first strips sewn will be stitched from top to bottom. The next strip will be sewn on from bottom to top. This helps the strip sets lay flat and even. To save time and thread, these strips sets are sewn continuously without cutting the thread at the end of the strip. Follow the steps below when sewing strip sets.

Example: Row 1. Pick up the top strip from the pile labeled Row 1. Pin the Row 1 label on the right side, upper left corner of this strip.

Lay the first and second strips right sides together, with the second strip on top. Stitch the seam.

Do not cut the thread, but pull out about 6" of thread. Bring the top ends of the strips (where you began stitching) into your lap. Open the two strips just stitched. Layer the third strip and the second strip, right sides together, with the second strip on top. Stitch.

Continue adding strips in this manner until all the strips are added for the Row 1 strip set. Always keep even numbered strips (2, 4, etc.) on top and odd numbered strips on the bottom.

Stitch the remaining strip set rows in the same manner.

Pressing

Lay a strip set, seam side up, on the ironing surface. Press the seams toward the first strip sewn (it has the label pinned to it).

I prefer to steam press. Press gently and let the steam do the work. Remember you are pressing, not ironing. To press, lift the iron and move it to another area. Don't push and pull the iron across the surface. Use little or no pressure on the iron. When all seams are pressed toward the label, flip the strip set over to the right side. Press, making sure no little folds have been pressed on the right side of the strip set. Repeat with all the strip sets.

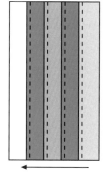

Slicing

Cut the strip sets into 1-1/2" slices. Cut one slice, per row, for each block in the quilt. Some quilts use extra slices of the first or last row to balance the design. The specific quilt directions give you this information. Lay the strip set horizontally on the cutting mat. Lay the ruler on the strip set, placing the long edge of the ruler parallel to the selvage edge of the strip set and a line on the ruler along one of the seams. Trim the selvages from the strip set. Place the 1-1/2" line on the ruler along this cut edge. Cut along the edge of the ruler to cut a slice.

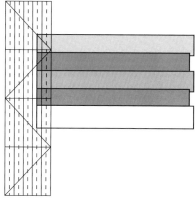

Lay the slices in piles for each row, with the label on top.

Blocks

Pulling the Blocks

"Pulling the blocks" means to gather a stack of slices which will be sewn into a block. Lay a slice from Row 1 on the table, seam allowances down. Place a slice from each row on top, ending with Row 10 (Row 12 for a 12" block).

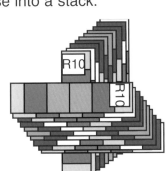

Lay this pile on the table. Repeat for each block in the quilt. Lay each block pile crosswise into a stack.

Sewing the Blocks

Pick up the first block pile and turn it over so the seam allowances face you. Lay the Row 1 slice right side up on the sewing machine. Place the Row 2 slice on top, with right sides together. There are no seam allowances to match. Stitch the seam. Clip the thread and open. Lay the third slice on top of the second, right sides together, and stitch. Clip thread and continue adding slices until the block is complete. All seams are stitched in the same direction. Repeat for all the blocks.

Assembly

Sewing Rows

Once all the blocks are stitched, sew them into rows. When the blocks are arranged with the strip set rows running horizontally in the quilt, they are sewn together in vertical rows. When the strip set rows run vertically in the quilt, the blocks are sewn together in horizontal rows. Each quilt will state which setting is used. Press the seams in odd rows (1, 3, etc.) toward the last strip set row. Press the seams in even rows toward the first strip set row.

Joining Rows

Lay the first row right side up. Lay the second row on top, right sides together. The seam allowances should be going in opposite directions. They will nest together where they meet, making matching seams a breeze. You may pin at each seam intersection, if necessary. Stitch the seam. Repeat for each row.

Borders

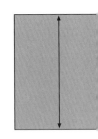

Plain Borders

Sew the 44" border strips together, end to end. Measure the quilt in the center, top to bottom.

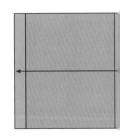

Cut the side borders this measurement and sew to the sides of the quilt. Press the seam allowance toward the border. Measure the quilt in the center, side to side, including the side borders.

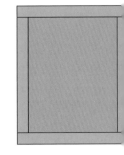

Cut the top and bottom borders this measurements. Sew to the quilt and press

Optional Strip Pieced Borders

Strip pieced borders may replace the 4-1/2" border on any of the quilts. The quilt, Rrribbit, page 34, has a pieced border. Four or more fabrics are used to piece the border. Purchase the total amount below instead of that shown on the yardage charts for the 4-1/2" border.

Wall - 1 yd. total, 2 strip sets
Lap - 2 yds. total, 4 strip sets
Twin/Full/Qn - 2-1/2 yds. total, 5 strip sets
King - 3 yds. total, 6 strip sets

Choose one of the border fabrics to be used in the corners. Cut a 4-1/2" strip from this fabric. Slice it into four 4-1/2" slices. Set aside.

Cut the remaining fabric into 1-1/2" strips, including the leftovers from the 4-1/2" strip. Counter-stitch eight strips into a strip set. Sew together the number of strip sets indicated above. Sew the strips together in a repeating order or place them randomly. Press the seams toward the darkest fabrics. Cut 4-1/2" slices from the strip sets. Each strip set will yield 8 to 9 slices.

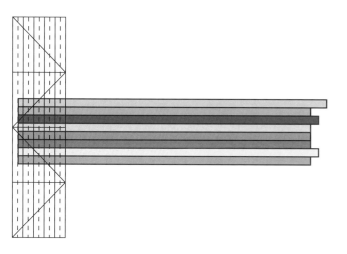

Stitch together enough slices to make two borders the length of the quilt. Also stitch together slices to make two borders the width of the quilt. Sew the side borders on. Add a 4-1/2" square at each end of the top and bottom borders. Stitch the top and bottom borders on, lining up the 4-1/2" squares with the side borders. Press the pieced border toward the plain border.

Finishing

Pressing and Backing

Press the completed top so all seams are laying flat.

Assemble the backing for the quilt according to the diagrams shown at right. Press backing seams toward the outside edge of the quilt.

Prepare Batting

Purchase batting large enough so it will be at least 4" longer and wider than the quilt top. Remove it from the package and let it lay unfolded for at least 12 hours or prepare it according to the package instructions. This will help it lay flat when assembling the quilt.

Quilting

These quilts may be machine or hand quilted. Quilt them to enhance the design or in the ditch. If you need help with the basting or quilting process refer to a book on quilting or a quilt shop.

Bindings

Yardage is based on binding strips cut crosswise from 44" fabric. Up to 3" wide strips may be cut. Wider bindings require more fabric. Sew the strips together end to end and press in half lengthwise. Attach the binding using your favorite method.

Label

Make a label with the quilt name, your name, place made and date made. If the quilt is a gift, include that information. Relatives and researchers a hundred years from now will thank you for documenting your quilt.

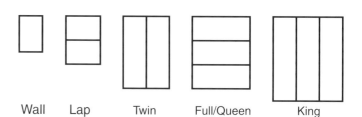

Wall   Lap   Twin   Full/Queen   King

DANCING DIAMONDS

Notice the diamond in the center of the block. This quilt is striking when a light tone on tone background fabric is used for the paths. The darkest fabric forms the outside of the diamonds. Two different fabrics, Center "A" and Center "B", are the diamond centers.

The drawing shows a queen size with three borders, the photographed quilt has only two borders.

Photo on page 23
10" block
Vertical Setting

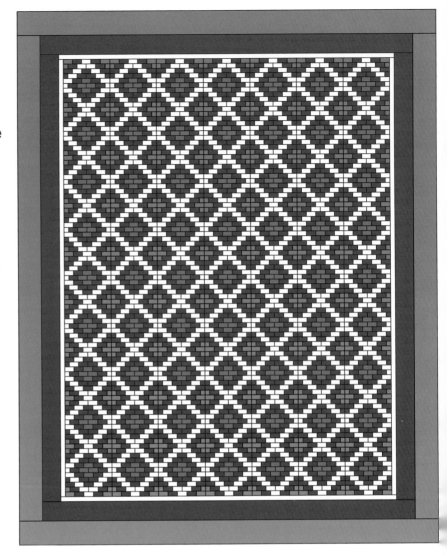

Yardage

		Wall 40" x 41" 9 blocks (3 x 3)	Lap 50" x 61" 20 blocks (4 x 5)	Twin 70" x 101" 40 blocks (5 x 8)	Full 84" x 105" 63 blocks (7 x 9)	Queen 90" x 111" 63 blocks (7 x 9)	King 110" x 111" 81 blocks (9 x 9)
Background		3/4	1-1/2	2-7/8	4-1/4	4-1/4	5
Darkest		1	1-7/8	3-3/4	5-5/8	5-5/8	6-5/8
Center "A"		1/4	1/3	5/8	1	1	1-1/8
Center "B"		1/4	3/8	3/4	1	1	1-1/4
Border # 1		1/4	1/4	1/3	3/8	3/8	1/2
Border # 2		5/8	3/4	1	3/4	1-1/4	1-3/8
Border # 3				1-3/8	1-1/4	1-3/4	1-7/8
Binding		3/8	5/8	7/8	1	1	1-1/8
Backing		1-1/4	3-1/8	6	7-5/8	8	9-7/8

Cutting

	Wall	Lap	Twin	Full	Queen	King
Background						
2-1/2"	9	17	34	51	51	60
1-1/2"	1	2	4	6	6	7
Darkest						
2-1/2"	11	22	44	66	66	77
1-1/2"	2	4	8	12	12	14
Center "A"						
2-1/2"	2	4	8	12	12	14
Center "B"						
2-1/2"	1	2	4	6	6	7
1-1/2"	2	4	8	12	12	14
Border # 1						
1-1/2"	4	5	7	8	8	9
Border # 2						
4-1/2"	4	5	7		9	10
2-1/2"				9		
Border # 3						
5-1/2"				8		10	11
4-1/2"					9	
Binding						
3"	4	6	9	10	10	11

Strip Sets

	Wall	Lap	Twin	Full	Queen	King
of strip sets	1/2	1	2	3	3	3-1/2

Once the blocks are assembled into rows, add a slice from Strip Set 1 to the bottom of each to balance the design.

Row 1

2-1/2" Center "B"
2-1/2" Darkest
2-1/2" B'grnd
2-1/2" Darkest
2-1/2" Center "B"

Rows 2 & 10

1-1/2" Center "B"
2-1/2" Darkest
2-1/2" B'grnd
2-1/2" B'grnd
2-1/2" Darkest
1-1/2" Center "B"

Rows 3 & 9

2-1/2" Darkest
2-1/2" B'grnd
2-1/2" Darkest
2-1/2" B'grnd
2-1/2" Darkest

Rows 4 & 8

1-1/2" Darkest
2-1/2" B'grnd
2-1/2" Darkest
2-1/2" Darkest
2-1/2" B'grnd
1-1/2" Darkest

Rows 5 & 7

2-1/2" B-grnd
2-1/2" Darkest
2-1/2" Center "A"
2-1/2" Darkest
2-1/2" B'grnd

Row 6

1-1/2" B'grnd
2-1/2" Darkest
2-1/2" Center "A"
2-1/2" Center "A"
2-1/2" Darkest
1-1/2" B'grnd

THE WAVE

The block by block assembly makes this wave easy to stitch.

Color family "A" has a light, a medium, and a dark. Color family "B" has a medium light and a medium dark. The design also looks good when shaded from light to dark across the quilt. For a bold look, use highly contrasting fabrics. This is a fun quilt to experiment with.

Photo on Back Cover
10" block
Vertical Setting

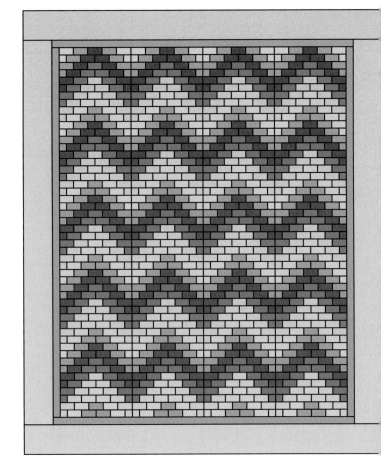

Yardage

		Wall 40" x 40" 9 blocks (3 x 3)	Lap 50" x 60" 20 blocks (4 x 5)	Twin 70" x 100" 40 blocks (5 x 8)	Full 84" x 104" 63 blocks (7 x 9)	Queen 90" x 110" 63 blocks (7 x 9)	King 110" x 110" 81 blocks (9 x 9)
Color "A" light		1/2	7/8	1-5/8	2-1/3	2-1/3	2-7/8
Color "A" medium		1/2	7/8	1-5/8	2-1/3	2-1/3	2-7/8
Color "A" dark		1/2	7/8	1-5/8	2-1/3	2-1/3	2-7/8
Color "B" med lt		1/2	7/8	1-5/8	2-1/3	2-1/3	2-7/8
Color "B" med dk		1/2	7/8	1-5/8	2-1/3	2-1/3	2-7/8
Border # 1		1/4	1/4	1/3	3/8	3/8	1/2
Border # 2		5/8	3/4	1	3/4	1-1/4	1-3/8
Border # 3				1-3/8	1-1/4	1-3/4	1-7/8
Binding		3/8	5/8	7/8	1	1	1-1/8
Backing		1-1/4	3-1/8	6	7-5/8	8	9-7/8

utting

	Wall	Lap	Twin	Full	Queen	King
olor "A" light						
2-1/2"	5	9	18	27	27	32
1-1/2"	1	2	4	6	6	7
olor "A" medium						
2-1/2"	5	9	18	27	27	32
1-1/2"	1	2	4	6	6	7
olor "A" dark						
2-1/2"	5	9	18	27	27	32
1-1/2"	1	2	4	6	6	7
olor "B" med lt						
2-1/2"	5	9	18	27	27	32
1-1/2"	1	2	4	6	6	7
olor "B" med dk						
2-1/2"	5	9	18	27	27	32
1-1/2"	1	2	4	6	6	7
order # 1						
1-1/2"	4	5	7	8	8	9
order # 2						
4-1/2"	4	5	7		9	10
2-1/2"				9		
order # 3						
5-1/2"			8		10	11
4-1/2"				9		
inding						
3"	4	6	9	10	10	11

trip Sets

	Wall	Lap	Twin	Full	Queen	King
of strip sets	1/2	1	2	3	3	3-1/2

Row 1
2-1/2" "A" light
2-1/2" "A" med
2-1/2" "B" m. dk
2-1/2" "A" med
2-1/2" "A" light

Row 2
1-1/2" "A" light
2-1/2" "A" med
2-1/2" "B" m. dk
2-1/2" "B" m. dk
2-1/2" "A" med
1-1/2" "A" light

Row 3
2-1/2" "A" med
2-1/2" "B" m. dk
2-1/2" "A" dark
2-1/2" "B" m. dk
2-1/2" "A" med

Row 4
1-1/2" "A" med
2-1/2" "B" m. dk
2-1/2" "A" dark
2-1/2" "A" dark
2-1/2" "B" m. dk
1-1/2" "A" med

Row 5
2-1/2" "B" med dk
2-1/2" "A" dark
2-1/2" "B" med lt
2-1/2" "A" dark
2-1/2" "B" med dk

Row 6
1-1/2" "B" med dk
2-1/2" "A" dark
2-1/2" "B" med lt
2-1/2" "B" med lt
2-1/2" "A" dark
1-1/2" "B" med dk

Row 7
2-1/2" "A" dark
2-1/2" "B" med lt
2-1/2" "A" light
2-1/2" "B" med lt
2-1/2" "A" dark

Row 8
1-1/2" "A" dark
2-1/2" "B" med lt
2-1/2" "A" light
2-1/2" "A" light
2-1/2" "B" med lt
1-1/2" "A" dark

Row 9
2-1/2" "B" med lt
2-1/2" "A" light
2-1/2" "A" medium
2-1/2" "A" light
2-1/2" "B" med lt

Row 10
1-1/2" "B" med lt
2-1/2" "A" light
2-1/2" "A" medium
2-1/2" "A" medium
2-1/2" "A" light
1-1/2" "B" med lt

11

CALL OF THE WILD

The right fabrics make this a great masculine quilt. It is a variation of the Wave, page 10. Select a background. Colors "A" and "B" form the diamonds. Add color "C" to run as a zig zag through the design.

Assembling the blocks into rows is different for this quilt. Sew the blocks together in mirror-image pairs. Simply follow the diagram. These blocks are turned 90° so the 1-1/2" slices run in vertical rows. They are stitched together in horizontal rows.

10" block
Horizontal Setting

Yardage

		Wall 30" x 30" 4 blocks (2 x 2)	Lap 50" x 60" 20 blocks (4 x 5)	Twin 70" x 100" 40 blocks (5 x 8)	Full 84" x 104" 63 blocks (7 x 9)	Queen 90" x 110" 63 blocks (7 x 9)	King 110" x 110" 81 blocks (9 x 9)
Background		5/8	2-1/8	4-1/8	6-1/8	6-1/8	7-1/4
Color "A"		1/4	5/8	1-1/8	1-5/8	1-5/8	2
Color "B"		1/4	5/8	1-1/8	1-2/3	1-2/3	2
Color "C"		1/3	7/8	1-5/8	2-3/8	2-3/8	2-7/8
Border # 1		1/4	1/4	1/3	3/8	3/8	1/2
Border # 2		1/2	3/4	1	3/4	1-1/4	1-3/8
Border # 3				1-3/8	1-1/4	1-3/4	1-7/8
Binding		3/8	5/8	7/8	1	1	1-1/8
Backing		1	3-1/8	6	7-5/8	8	9-7/8

Cutting

	Wall	Lap	Twin	Full	Queen	King
Background ▢						
2-1/2"	6	23	46	69	69	81
1-1/2"	2	6	12	18	18	21
Color "A" ▢						
2-1/2"	2	7	14	21	21	25
Color "B" ▢						
2-1/2"	2	6	12	18	18	21
1-1/2"	1	2	4	6	6	7
Color "C" ▢						
2-1/2"	3	9	18	27	27	32
1-1/2"	1	2	4	6	6	7
Border # 1						
1-1/2"	3	5	7	8	8	9
Border # 2						
4-1/2"	3	5	7		9	10
2-1/2"				9		
Border # 3						
5-1/2"			8		10	11
4-1/2"				9		
Binding						
3"	4	6	9	10	10	11

Strip Sets

	Wall	Lap	Twin	Full	Queen	King
# of strip sets	1/4	1	2	3	3	3-1/2

Row 1

2-1/2" B'grnd
2-1/2" "B"
2-1/2" B'grnd
2-1/2" "B"
2-1/2" B'grnd

Row 2

1-1/2" B'grnd
2-1/2" "B"
2-1/2" B'grnd
2-1/2" B'grnd
2-1/2" "B"
1-1/2" B'grnd

Row 3

2-1/2" "B"
2-1/2" B'grnd
2-1/2" "C"
2-1/2" B'grnd
2-1/2" "B"

Row 4

1-1/2" "B"
2-1/2" B'grnd
2-1/2" "C"
2-1/2" "C"
2-1/2" B'grnd
1-1/2" "B"

Row 5

2-1/2" B'grnd
2-1/2" "C"
2-1/2" B'grnd
2-1/2" "C"
2-1/2" B'grnd

Row 6

1-1/2" B'grnd
2-1/2" "C"
2-1/2" B'grnd
2-1/2" B'grnd
2-1/2" "C"
1-1/2" B'grnd

Row 7

2-1/2" "C"
2-1/2" B'grnd
2-1/2" "A"
2-1/2" B'grnd
2-1/2" "C"

Row 8

1-1/2" "C"
2-1/2" B'grnd
2-1/2" "A"
2-1/2" "A"
2-1/2" B'grnd
1-1/2" "C"

Row 9

2-1/2" B'grnd
2-1/2" "A"
2-1/2" B'grnd
2-1/2" "A"
2-1/2" B'grnd

Row 10

1-1/2" B'grnd
2-1/2" "A"
2-1/2" B'grnd
2-1/2" B'grnd
2-1/2" "A"
1-1/2" B'grnd

MORE DANCING DIAMONDS

Look at how the background fabrics weave through the diamonds. Two dark or two light fabrics, #1 and #2, are used to make the background crossing paths. Example: A black solid and a black on black print, or a cream solid and a cream on cream print. Two color families are used for the diamonds. The diamonds are a dark and a medium light from color family A, and a dark and a medium light from color family B.

Photo on page 21
10" Block
Vertical Setting

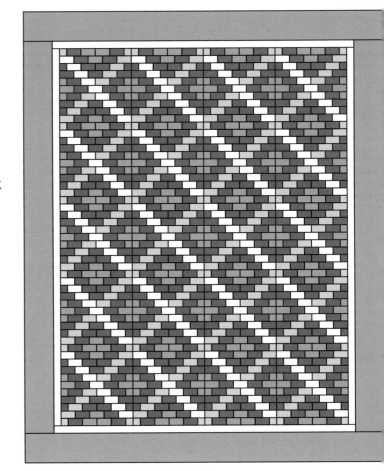

Yardage

		Wall 40" x 41" 9 blocks (3 x 3)	Lap 50" x 61" 20 blocks (4 x 5)	Twin 70" x 101" 40 blocks (5 x 8)	Full 84" x 105" 63 blocks (7 x 9)	Queen 90" x 111" 63 blocks (7 x 9)	King 110" x 111" 81 blocks (9 x 9)
Background # 1		1/2	3/4	1-3/8	2-1/8	2-1/8	2-1/2
Background # 2		3/8	3/4	1-1/2	2-1/8	2-1/8	2-1/2
Color "A" dark		1/2	1	1-7/8	2-3/4	2-3/4	3-1/4
Color "A" med. light		1/4	1/3	5/8	1	1	1-1/8
Color "B" dark		1/2	1	2	2-7/8	2-7/8	3-1/3
Color "B" med. light		1/4	3/8	3/4	1-1/8	1-1/8	1-1/4
Border #1		1/4	1/4	1/3	3/8	3/8	1/2
Border # 2		5/8	3/4	1	3/4	1-1/4	1-3/8
Border # 3				1-3/8	1-1/4	1-3/4	1-7/8
Binding		3/8	5/8	7/8	1	1	1-1/8
Backing		1-1/4	3-1/8	6	7-5/8	8	9-7/8

14

Cutting

		Wall	Lap	Twin	Full	Queen	King
Background # 1							
2-1/2"		5	9	18	27	27	32
Background # 2							
2-1/2"		4	8	16	24	24	28
1-1/2"		1	2	4	6	6	7
Color "A" dark							
2-1/2"		6	12	24	36	36	42
Color "A" med. light							
2-1/2"		2	4	8	12	12	14
Color "B" dark							
2-1/2"		5	10	20	30	30	35
1-1/2"		2	4	8	12	12	14
Color "B" med. light							
2-1/2"		1	2	4	6	6	7
1-1/2"		2	4	8	12	12	14
Border #1							
1-1/2"		4	5	7	8	8	9
Border # 2							
4-1/2"		4	5	7		9	10
2-1/2"					9		
Border # 3							
5-1/2"				8		10	11
4-1/2"					9		
Binding							
3"		4	6	9	10	10	11

Strip Sets

	Wall	Lap	Twin	Full	Queen	King
of strip sets	1/2	1	2	3	3	3-1/2

Notice that Rows 6, 7, 8, and 9 are identical to Rows 4, 3, 2, and 1 but are turned 180°. Press the seam toward the strip which is on the left in the block.

After the blocks are assembled into rows, add an additional slice from Strip Set 10 to the top of each row, see drawing, to balance the design.

Rows 1 & 9

2-1/2" B'grnd 1
2-1/2" "A" dark
2-1/2" "A" med lt
2-1/2" "A" dark
2-1/2" B'grnd 2

Rows 2 & 8

1-1/2" "B" dark
2-1/2" B'grnd 1
2-1/2" "A" dark
2-1/2" "A" dark
2-1/2" B'grnd 2
1-1/2" "B" dark

Rows 3 & 7

2-1/2" "B" dark
2-1/2" B'grnd 1
2-1/2" "A" dark
2-1/2" B'grnd 2
2-1/2" "B" dark

Rows 4 & 6

1-1/2" "B" med lt
2-1/2" "B" dark
2-1/2" B'grnd 1
2-1/2" B'grnd 2
2-1/2" "B" dark
1-1/2" "B" med lt

Row 5

2-1/2" "B" med lt
2-1/2" "B" dark
2-1/2" B'grnd 1
2-1/2" "B" dark
2-1/2" "B" med lt

Row 10

1-1/2" B'grnd 2
2-1/2" "A" dark
2-1/2" "A" med lt
2-1/2" "A" med lt
2-1/2" "A" dark
1-1/2" B'grnd 2

Variations of Dancing Diamonds

One Rotten Apple in the Basket
Spoils the Whole Bunch - page 17

Backgrounds #1 and #2 are the same in this version. One fabric is used for the paths. The diamonds are reverse of each other, fabrics "A" dark and "B" medium light are the same as are "A" medium light and "B" dark. Simply combine yardage from the chart when purchasing fabric.

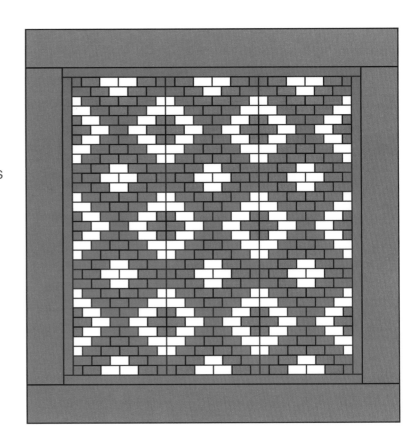

Amish Dancing Diamonds

This variation also uses one fabric for the paths. Combine the yardage for backgrounds #1 and #2. The diamonds are made with two color families as explained on page 14.

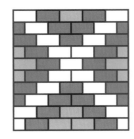

Christmas Wreath
41" x 41"

One Rotten Apple in the Basket
40" x 41"
by Shirley Hassler, Columbus, NE

Mosaic
50" x 58"

Rrribbit

58" x 70"

Straight Furrows

50" x 60"

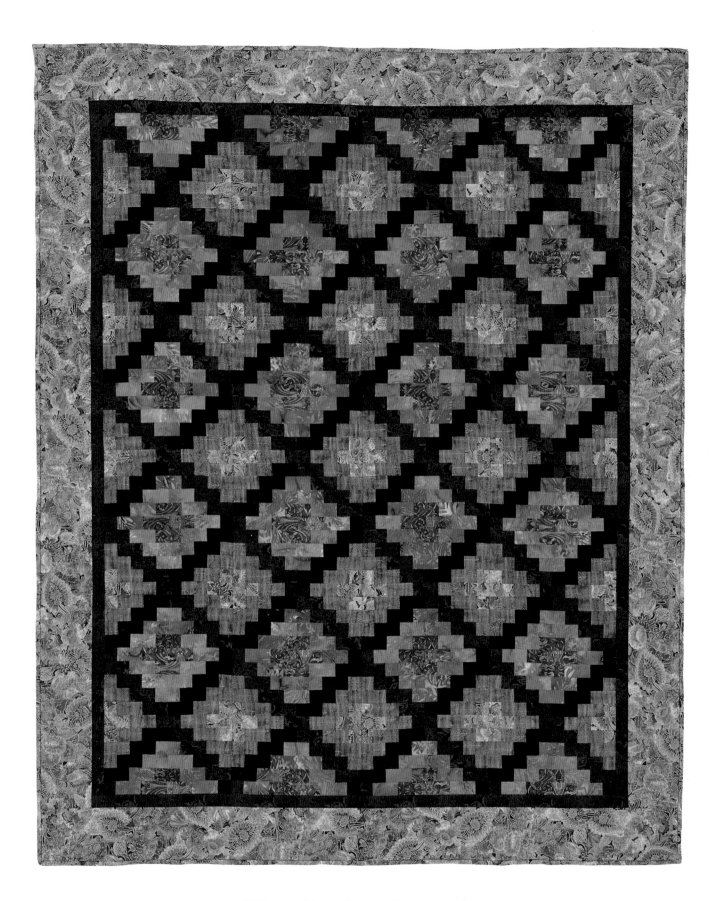

More Dancing Diamonds
50" x 61"

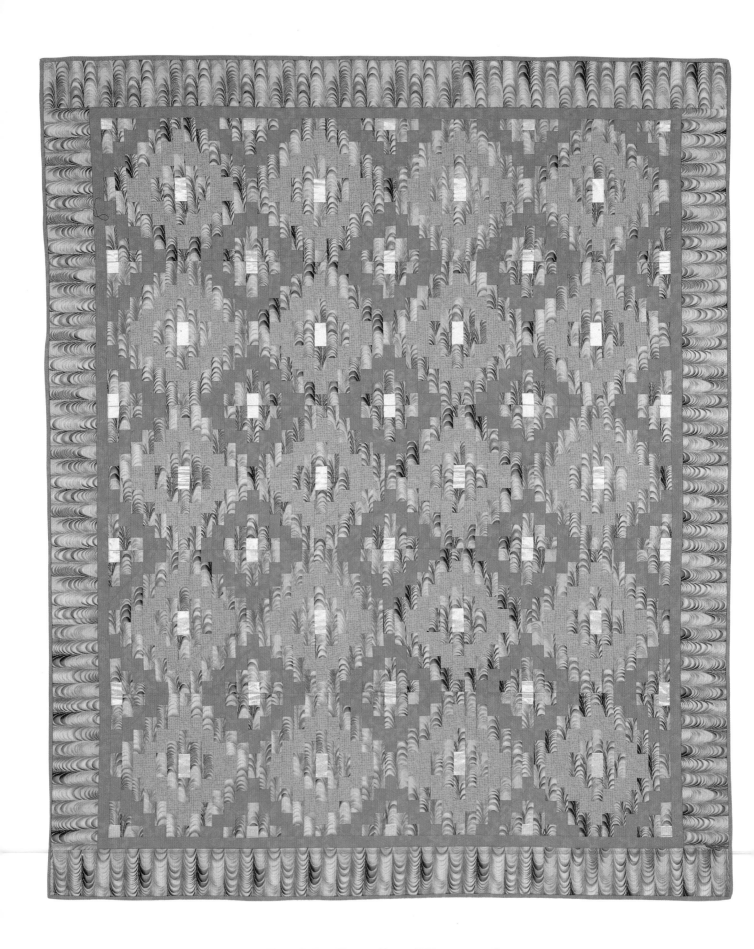

Double Dancing Diamonds

59" x 70"

Dancing Diamonds
80" x 101"

STRAIGHT FURROWS

As the name suggests, this variation has diagonal rows across the quilt. The photographed quilt uses a light and a medium of Color "A", and a medium and a dark of Color "B". Color "C" has both colors in it.

This design is subtle if the values of the fabrics are close. When the values are close, and prints and florals are used, a watercolor effect is achieved. Highly contrasting fabrics result in a bold look.

Photo on page 20
10" block
Horizontal Setting

Yardage

		Wall 40" x 40" 9 blocks (3 x 3)	Lap 50" x 60" 20 blocks (4 x 5)	Twin 70" x 100" 40 blocks (5 x 8)	Full 84" x 104" 63 blocks (7 x 9)	Queen 90" x 110" 63 blocks (7 x 9)	King 110" x 110" 81 blocks (9 x 9)
Color "A" Light		1/2	7/8	1-5/8	2-1/3	2-1/3	2-7/8
Medium		1/2	7/8	1-5/8	2-1/3	2-1/3	2-7/8
Color "B" Medium		1/2	7/8	1-5/8	2-1/3	2-1/3	2-7/8
Dark		1/2	7/8	1-5/8	2-1/3	2-1/3	2-7/8
Color "C"		1/2	7/8	1-5/8	2-1/3	2-1/3	2-7/8
Border # 1		1/4	1/4	1/3	3/8	3/8	1/2
Border # 2		5/8	3/4	1	3/4	1-1/4	1-3/8
Border # 3				1-3/8	1-1/4	1-3/4	1-7/8
Binding		3/8	5/8	7/8	1	1	1-1/8
Backing		1-1/4	3-1/8	6	7-5/8	8	9-7/8

Cutting

	Wall	Lap	Twin	Full	Queen	King
Color "A" Light						
2-1/2"	5	9	18	27	27	32
1-1/2"	1	2	4	6	6	7
Color "A" Medium						
2-1/2"	5	9	18	27	27	32
1-1/2"	1	2	4	6	6	7
Color "B" Medium						
2-1/2"	5	9	18	27	27	32
1-1/2"	1	2	4	6	6	7
Color "B" Dark						
2-1/2"	5	9	18	27	27	32
1-1/2"	1	2	4	6	6	7
Color "C"						
2-1/2"	5	9	18	27	27	32
1-1/2"	1	2	4	6	6	7
Border # 1						
1-1/2"	4	5	7	8	8	9
Border # 2						
4-1/2"	4	5	7		9	10
2-1/2"				9		
Border # 3						
5-1/2"			8		10	11
4-1/2"				9		
Binding						
3"	4	6	9	10	10	11

Strip Sets

	Wall	Lap	Twin	Full	Queen	King
# of strip sets	1/2	1	2	3	3	3-1/2

Row 1

2-1/2" "A" lt
2-1/2" "C"
2-1/2" "B" med
2-1/2" "B" dk
2-1/2" "A" med

Row 2

1-1/2" "A" lt
2-1/2" "C"
2-1/2" "B" med
2-1/2" "B" dk
2-1/2" "A" med
1-1/2" "A" lt

Row 3

2-1/2" "C"
2-1/2" "B" med
2-1/2" "B" dk
2-1/2" "A" med
2-1/2" "A" lt

Row 4

1-1/2" "C"
2-1/2" "B" med
2-1/2" "B" dk
2-1/2" "A" med
2-1/2" "A" lt
1-1/2" "C"

Row 5

2-1/2" "B" med
2-1/2" "B" dk
2-1/2" "A" med
2-1/2" "A" lt
2-1/2" "C"

Row 6

1-1/2" "B" med
2-1/2" "B" dk
2-1/2" "A" med
2-1/2" "A" lt
2-1/2" "C"
1-1/2" "B" med

Row 7

2-1/2" "B" dk
2-1/2" "A" med
2-1/2" "A" lt
2-1/2" "C"
2-1/2" "B" med

Row 8

1-1/2" "B" dk
2-1/2" "A" med
2-1/2" "A" lt
2-1/2" "C"
2-1/2" "B" med
1-1/2" "B" dk

Row 9

2-1/2" "A" med
2-1/2" "A" lt
2-1/2" "C"
2-1/2" "B" med
2-1/2" "B" dk

Row 10

1-1/2" "A" med
2-1/2" "A" lt
2-1/2" "C"
2-1/2" "B" med
2-1/2" "B" dk
1-1/2" "A" med

MOROCCAN TILES

Try different color schemes with this design. It works well in Southwest or Oriental colors. Select five fabrics in two color families with strong contrast. In Color "A", choose a dark and a light. Choose a dark, a medium, and a light in Color "B".

Once the blocks are assembled into rows, add a slice of Strip Set 1 to the bottom of each to balance the design.

10" block
Vertical Setting

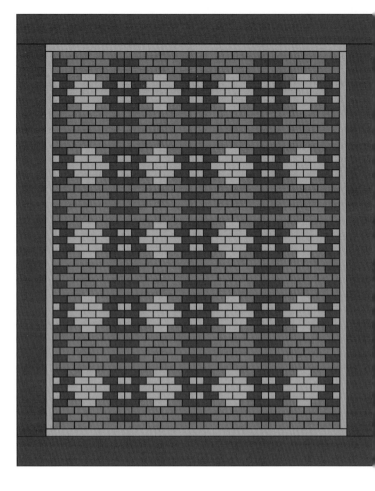

Yardage

		Wall 40" x 41" 9 blocks (3 x 3)	Lap 50" x 61" 20 blocks (4 x 5)	Twin 70" x 101" 40 blocks (5 x 8)	Full 84" x 105" 63 blocks (7 x 9)	Queen 90" x 111" 63 blocks (7 x 9)	King 110" x 111" 81 blocks (9 x 9)
Color "A"							
Dark		1/2	1	1-7/8	2-3/4	2-3/4	3-1/4
Light		1/4	1/3	5/8	7/8	7/8	1
Color "B"							
Dark		5/8	1-1/8	2-1/4	3-1/4	3-1/4	3-3/4
Medium		5/8	1-1/8	2-1/8	3-1/8	3-1/8	3-2/3
Light		1/3	5/8	1-1/4	1-7/8	1-7/8	2-1/4
Border # 1		1/4	1/4	1/3	3/8	3/8	1/2
Border # 2		5/8	3/4	1	3/4	1-1/4	1-3/8
Border # 3				1-3/8	1-1/4	1-3/4	1-7/8
Binding		3/8	5/8	7/8	1	1	1-1/8
Backing		1-1/4	3-1/8	6	7-5/8	8	9-7/8

Cutting

		Wall	Lap	Twin	Full	Queen	King
Color "A" Dark							
2-1/2"		6	12	24	36	36	42
Color "A" Light							
2-1/2"		1	1	2	3	3	4
1-1/2"		2	4	8	12	12	14
Color "B" Dark							
2-1/2"		7	14	28	42	42	49
Color "B" Medium							
2-1/2"		5	10	20	30	30	35
1-1/2"		3	6	12	18	18	21
Color "B" Light							
2-1/2"		4	8	16	24	24	28
Border # 1							
1-1/2"		4	5	7	8	8	9
Border # 2							
4-1/2"		4	5	7		9	10
2-1/2"					9		
Border # 3							
5-1/2"				8		10	11
4-1/2"					9		
Binding							
3"		4	6	9	10	10	11

Strip Sets

	Wall	Lap	Twin	Full	Queen	King
of strip sets	1/2	1	2	3	3	3-1/2

Rows 1, 3, & 9

1-1/2" "B" medium
2-1/2" "B" medium
2-1/2" "A" dark
2-1/2" "A" dark
2-1/2" "B" medium
1-1/2" "B" medium

Rows 2 & 10

2-1/2" "B" dark
2-1/2" "B" medium
2-1/2" "A" dark
2-1/2" "B" medium
2-1/2" "B" dark

Rows 4 & 8

2-1/2" "B" dark
2-1/2" "A" dark
2-1/2" "B" light
2-1/2" "A" dark
2-1/2" "B" dark

Rows 5 & 7

1-1/2" "A" light
2-1/2" "B" dark
2-1/2" "B" light
2-1/2" "B" light
2-1/2" "B" dark
1-1/2" "A" light

Row 6

2-1/2" "B" dark
2-1/2" "B" light
2-1/2" "A" light
2-1/2" "B" light
2-1/2" "B" dark

CHRISTMAS WREATH

A fun wall quilt to hang for the holidays! It is made with nine blocks surrounded by background fabric. Select a wreath fabric, a bow fabric, a background, and a second background for the center of the wreath.

Use half strip sets to make the rows. Remember, a half strip set is made with strips that are 21" - 22" in length.

Photo on page 17
10" block

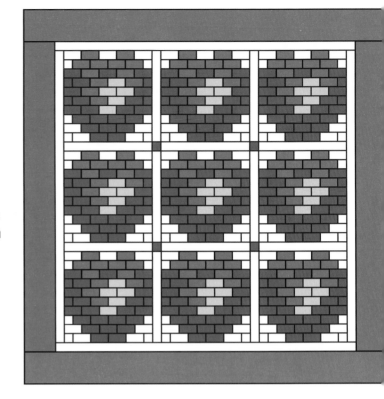

Yardage

		Wall 41" x 41" 9 blocks (3 x 3)
Wreath	■	1
Bow	■	1/2
Background	□	7/8
Background #2	▨	1/4
Border # 2		1/2
Binding		3/8
Backing		1-1/3 Tight!

Assembly Notes:

Build nine blocks using the strip sets at the right.

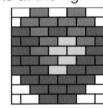

This quilt uses sashing. Sew the blocks together into three horizontal rows with 1-1/2" x 10-1/2" sashing strips between.

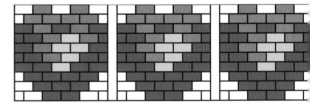

Sew two horizontal sashing rows using three 1-1/2" x 10-1/2" sashing strips and two 1-1/2" wreath squares for each.

Sew the rows of blocks together with the sashing rows between. Add the inner and outer border as explained in the general directions.

Cutting

		Wall
Wreath		
2-1/2"		11
1-1/2"		2
Bow		
2-1/2"		6
Background		
2-1/2"		4
1-1/2"		11
Background 2		
2-1/2"		3
Border # 2		
4"		4
Binding		
3"		4

Strip Sets

# of strip sets	1/2

Additional Cutting Information:

Wreath -
Cut the 2-1/2" strips in half for strip sets
There is one extra 2-1/2" x 22" half. Cut four 1-1/2" squares from it.
Cut the 1-1/2" strips in half for strip sets.

Bow -
Cut the 2-1/2" strips in half for strip sets.

Background -
Cut the 2-1/2" and three of the 1-1/2" strips in half for strip sets.
Cut four 1-1/2" strips into 10-1/2" lengths for sashing. Make 12.
Four 1-1/2" strips are for the inner border.

Background # 2 -
Cut the 2-1/2" strips in half for strip sets.

Row 1
2-1/2" B'grnd
2-1/2" Bow
2-1/2" B'grnd
2-1/2" Bow
2-1/2" B'grnd

Row 2
1-1/2" B'grnd
2-1/2" Bow
2-1/2" Bow
2-1/2" Bow
2-1/2" Bow
1-1/2" B'grnd

Row 3
2-1/2" Wreath
2-1/2" Bow
2-1/2" Wreath
2-1/2" Bow
2-1/2" Wreath

Row 4
1-1/2" Wreath
2-1/2" Wreath
2-1/2" Bow
2-1/2" B'grnd 2
2-1/2" Bow
1-1/2" Wreath

Row 5
2-1/2" Wreath
2-1/2" Bow
2-1/2" B'grnd 2
2-1/2" B'grnd 2
2-1/2" Wreath

Row 6
1-1/2" Wreath
2-1/2" Wreath
2-1/2" Bow
2-1/2" B'grnd 2
2-1/2" Wreath
1-1/2" Wreath

Row 7
2-1/2" Wreath
2-1/2" Wreath
2-1/2" B'grnd 2
2-1/2" Wreath
2-1/2" Wreath

Row 8
1-1/2" B'grnd
2-1/2" Wreath
2-1/2" Wreath
2-1/2" Wreath
2-1/2" Wreath
1-1/2" B'grnd

Row 9
2-1/2" B'grnd
2-1/2" Wreath
2-1/2" Wreath
2-1/2" Wreath
2-1/2" B'grnd

Row 10
1-1/2" B'grnd
1-1/2" B'grnd
2-1/2" Wreath
2-1/2" Wreath
2-1/2" B'grnd
1-1/2" B'grnd

29

DOUBLE DANCING DIAMONDS

Two rows of the background fabric are used to form the double diamond effect. Use either two contrasting fabrics or two color families for fabrics "A" and "B". An accent fabric, "C", is used in the centers. After the blocks are assembled into rows, add a slice of Strip Set 1 to the right end of each row.

Photo on page 22
12" block
Horizontal Setting

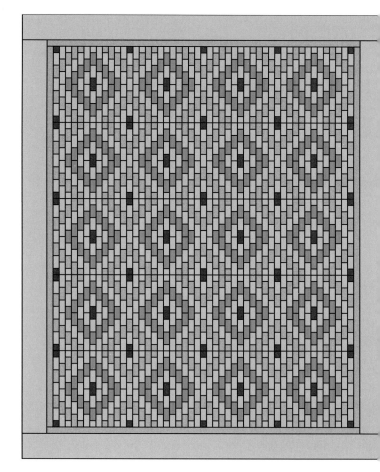

Yardage

		Wall 35" x 34" 4 blocks (2 x 2)	Lap 59" x 70" 20 blocks (4 x 5)	Twin 71" x 106" 40 blocks (5 x 8)	Full 85" x 108" 48 blocks (6 x 8)	Queen 93" x 116" 48 blocks (6 x 8)	King 109" x 108" 64 blocks (8 x 8)
Background		7/8	3	6	6-1/8	6-1/8	8-7/8
Color "A"		3/8	1-1/4	2-5/8	2-5/8	2-5/8	3-3/4
Color "B"		1/3	1-1/4	2-1/2	2-1/2	2-1/2	3-2/3
Color "C"		1/4	1/4	3/8	1/2	1/2	5/8
Border # 1		1/4	1/3	3/8	1/2	1/2	1/2
Border # 2		5/8	7/8	1-1/4	3/4	1-1/4	7/8
Border # 3					1	1-3/4	1-1/4
Binding		3/8	2/3	7/8	1	1-1/8	1-1/8
Backing		1-1/8	3-5/8	6-1/3	7-5/8	8-1/3	9-5/8

utting

	Wall	Lap	Twin	Full	Queen	King
Background						
2-1/2"	9	35	70	72	72	105
1-1/2"	2	6	12	12	12	18
Color "A"						
2-1/2"	4	14	28	29	29	42
1-1/2"	1	4	8	8	8	12
Color "B"						
2-1/2"	4	16	32	32	32	48
Color "C"						
2-1/2"	1	1	2	2	2	3
1-1/2"	1	2	4	5	5	6
Border # 1						
1-1/2"	4	6	8	9	9	10
Border # 2						
4-1/2"	4	6	9		9	
2-1/2"				9		10
Border # 3						
5-1/2"					10	
3-1/2"				9		11
Binding						
3"	4	7	9	10	11	11

trip Sets

of strip sets	1/4	1	2	2*	2*	3

Make 2-1/2 strip sets of Row 1 for the full and queen sizes.

Row 1

1-1/2" "C"
2-1/2" B'grnd
2-1/2" "A"
2-1/2" B'grnd
2-1/2" "A"
2-1/2" B'grnd
1-1/2" "C"

Rows 2 & 12

2-1/2" B'grnd
2-1/2" "A"
2-1/2" B'grnd
2-1/2" B'grnd
2-1/2" "A"
2-1/2" B'grnd

Rows 3 & 11

1-1/2" B'grnd
2-1/2" "A"
2-1/2" B'grnd
2-1/2" "B"
2-1/2" B'grnd
2-1/2" "A"
1-1/2" B'grnd

Rows 4 & 10

2-1/2" "A"
2-1/2" B'grnd
2-1/2" "B"
2-1/2" "B"
2-1/2" B'grnd
2-1/2" "A"

Rows 5 & 9

1-1/2" "A"
2-1/2" B'grnd
2-1/2" "B"
2-1/2" B'grnd
2-1/2" "B"
2-1/2" B'grnd
1-1/2" "A"

Rows 6 & 8

2-1/2" B'grnd
2-1/2" "B"
2-1/2" B'grnd
2-1/2" B'grnd
2-1/2" "B"
2-1/2" B'grnd

Row 7

1-1/2" B'grnd
2-1/2" "B"
2-1/2" B'grnd
2-1/2" "C"
2-1/2" B'grnd
2-1/2" "B"
1-1/2" B'grnd

31

LIGHTS 'N LANTERNS

A metallic lame' is used to represent the light inside the lantern. Graduating shades of orange and yellow were used for colors "A", "B", "C", and "D". Color "E" is dark, representing the outside rim of the lantern. Careful selection of colors could turn this lantern into a turkey quilt for Thanksgiving, or a peacock.

The blocks are rotated 90° before sewing together into horizontal rows. Notice that the photographed quilt, on the cover, has 12 blocks while our graphics show 20 blocks. Add a slice of Strip Set 1 to the right side of each row, see drawing, to balance the design.

Instructions for handling metallic lame' are on page 4.

Photo on Cover
12" block
Horizontal Setting

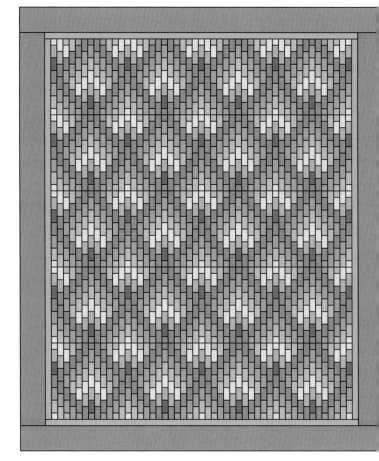

Yardage

		Wall 47" x 58" 12 blocks (3 x 4)	Lap 59" x 70" 20 blocks (4 x 5)	Twin 71" x 106" 40 blocks (5 x 8)	Full 85" x 108" 48 blocks (6 x 8)	Queen 93" x 116" 48 blocks (6 x 8)	King 109" x 108" 64 blocks (8 x 8)
Lame' *		1/4	1/4	1/3	1/2	1/2	1/2
Color "A"		1/3	1/2	1	1	1	1-3/8
Color "B"		1/2	7/8	1-5/8	1-5/8	1-5/8	2-1/3
Color "C"		2/3	1-1/8	2-1/4	2-1/3	2-1/3	3-1/3
Color "D"		7/8	1-1/2	2-7/8	3	3	4-1/4
Color "E"		1	1-3/4	3-1/2	3-1/2	3-1/2	5-1/8
Border # 1		1/4	1/3	3/8	1/2	1/2	1/2
Border # 2		3/4	7/8	1-1/4	3/4	1-1/4	7/8
Border # 3					1	1-3/4	1-1/4
Binding		5/8	2/3	7/8	1	1-1/8	1-1/8
Backing		3	3-5/8	6-1/3	7-5/8	8-1/3	9-5/8

* Purchase an equal amount of iron-on interfacing for lame'

utting

		Wall	Lap	Twin	Full	Queen	King
ame'							
2-1/2"		2	2	4	5	5	6
olor "A"							
2-1/2"		4	6	12	13	13	18
olor "B"							
2-1/2"		5	9	18	18	18	27
1-1/2"		2	2	4	5	5	6
olor "C"							
2-1/2"		7	12	24	25	25	36
1-1/2"		2	4	8	8	8	12
olor "D"							
2-1/2"		9	16	32	33	33	48
1-1/2"		2	4	8	8	8	12
olor "E"							
2-1/2"		11	21	42	43	43	63
1-1/2"		1	2	4	4	4	6
order # 1							
1-1/2"		5	6	8	9	9	10
order # 2							
4-1/2"		5	6	9		9	
2-1/2"					9		10
order # 3							
5-1/2"						10	
3-1/2"					9		11
inding							
3"		6	7	9	10	11	11

trip Sets

	Wall	Lap	Twin	Full	Queen	King
of strip sets	1/2*	1	2	2**	2**	3

* Make a full strip set of Row 1 for the wall size.

**Make 2-1/2 strip sets of Row 1 for the full and queen sizes.

Row 1

1-1/2" "B"
2-1/2" "C"
2-1/2" "D"
2-1/2" "E"
2-1/2" Lame'
2-1/2" "A"
1-1/2" "B"

Rows 2 & 12

2-1/2" "C"
2-1/2" "D"
2-1/2" "E"
2-1/2" "E"
2-1/2" "A"
2-1/2" "B"

Rows 3 & 11

1-1/2" "C"
2-1/2" "D"
2-1/2" "E"
2-1/2" "D"
2-1/2" "E"
2-1/2" "B"
1-1/2" "C"

Rows 4 & 10

2-1/2" "D"
2-1/2" "E"
2-1/2" "C"
2-1/2" "D"
2-1/2" "E"
2-1/2" "C"

Rows 5 & 9

1-1/2" "D"
2-1/2" "E"
2-1/2" "B"
2-1/2" "C"
2-1/2" "D"
2-1/2" "E"
1-1/2" "D"

Rows 6 & 8

2-1/2" "E"
2-1/2" "A"
2-1/2" "B"
2-1/2" "C"
2-1/2" "D"
2-1/2" "E"

Row 7

1-1/2" "E"
2-1/2" Lame'
2-1/2" "A"
2-1/2" "B"
2-1/2" "C"
2-1/2" "D"
1-1/2" "E"

RRRIBBIT

To get a large variety of frogs, a complete set of 1/4 strip sets is sewn for each six blocks needed. A 1/4 strip set is made with strips 1/4 the width of the fabric, about 11". Colors "A", "B", and "C" stay consistent throughout all the blocks. The remaining six fabrics change with each set of strip sets. Color "A" suggests a forest floor. The others are frogs. Colors "B" & "C" make complete frogs when the blocks are sewn into rows. Choose light colors for "B" through "E" and dark colors for "F" through "I".

Photo on page 19
12" block
Vertical Setting

NOTE: Yardage for colors "D" - "I" indicates the number of quarters needed. Fat quarters may be used, as well as pieces which are at least 11" x 22". The yardage given for the other fabric is the total needed.

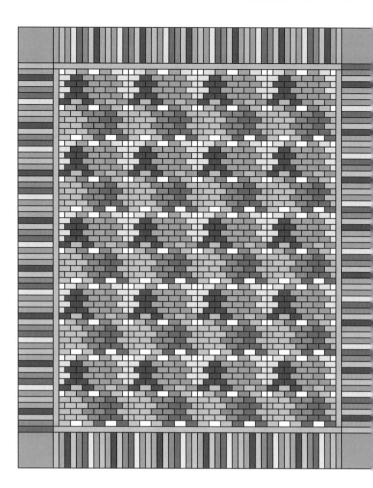

Yardage

		Wall 34" x 34" 4 blocks (2 x 2)	Lap 58" x 70" 20 blocks (4 x 5)	Twin 70" x 106" 40 blocks (5 x 8)	Full 84" x 108" 48 blocks (6 x 8)	Queen 92" x 116" 48 blocks (6 x 8)	King 108" x 108" 64 blocks (8 x 8)
Color "A" (forest)		1/4	1/2	7/8	1	1	1-3/8
Color "B" (light)		1/4	2/3	1-1/4	1-1/3	1-1/3	1-7/8
Color "C" (light)		1/4	7/8	1-1/2	1-5/8	1-5/8	2-1/4
Colors "D" & "E" total light quarters		2	8	14	16	16	22
Colors "F" - "I" total dark quarters		4	16	28	32	32	44
Border # 1		1/4	1/3	3/8	1/2	1/2	1/2
Border # 2		5/8	7/8	1-1/4	3/4	1-1/4	7/8
Border # 3					1	1-3/4	1-1/4
Binding		3/8	2/3	7/8	1	1-1/8	1-1/8
Backing		1-1/8	3-5/8	6-1/3	7-5/8	8-1/4	9-5/8

34

NOTE: The cutting chart indicates the number of full length strips to cut. Crosscut them into 1/4 strips, about 11". If you are working with fat quarters or scraps, cut four times as many 11" strips as full strips.

Cutting

	Wall	Lap	Twin	Full	Queen	King
Color "A"						
2-1/2"	1	4	7	8	8	11
1-1/2"	1	4	7	8	8	11
Color "B"						
2-1/2"	2	6	11	12	12	17
1-1/2"	1	4	7	8	8	11
Color "C"						
2-1/2"	2	8	14	16	16	22
1-1/2"	1	4	7	8	8	11

Colors "D" - "I"   D E F G H I
From EACH quarter - refer to page 34 for number of quarters to cut.

	Wall	Lap	Twin	Full	Queen	King
2-1/2"	2	2	2	2	2	2
Border # 1						
1-1/2"	4	6	8	9	9	10
Plain Border # 2*						
4-1/2"	4	6	9		9	
2-1/2"				9		10
Border # 3						
5-1/2"					10	
3-1/2"				9		11
Binding						
3"	4	7	9	10	11	11

Strip Sets

# of 1/4 strip sets	1	4	7	8	8	11

The featured quilt has a 4-1/2" pieced border. See page 6.

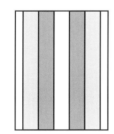

Row 1

1-1/2" "A"
2-1/2" "B"
2-1/2" "I"
2-1/2" "A"
2-1/2" "I"
2-1/2" "B"
1-1/2" "A"

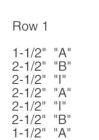

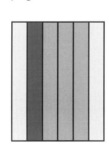

Rows 2 & 4

2-1/2" "B"
2-1/2" "F"
2-1/2" "I"
2-1/2" "I"
2-1/2" "E"
2-1/2" "B"

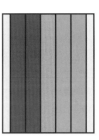

Rows 3 & 5

1-1/2" "B"
2-1/2" "F"
2-1/2" "F"
2-1/2" "I"
2-1/2" "E"
2-1/2" "E"
1-1/2" "B"

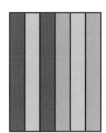

Row 6

2-1/2" "F"
2-1/2" "C"
2-1/2" "F"
2-1/2" "E"
2-1/2" "C"
2-1/2" "E"

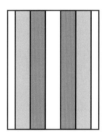

Row 7

1-1/2" "A"
2-1/2" "C"
2-1/2" "G"
2-1/2" "A"
2-1/2" "G"
2-1/2" "C"
1-1/2" "A"

Rows 8 & 10

2-1/2" "C"
2-1/2" "D"
2-1/2" "G"
2-1/2" "G"
2-1/2" "H"
2-1/2" "C"

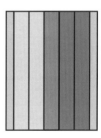

Rows 9 & 11

1-1/2" "C"
2-1/2" "D"
2-1/2" "D"
2-1/2" "G"
2-1/2" "H"
2-1/2" "H"
1-1/2" "C"

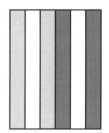

Row 12

2-1/2" "D"
2-1/2" "A"
2-1/2" "D"
2-1/2" "H"
2-1/2" "A"
2-1/2" "H"

MOSAIC

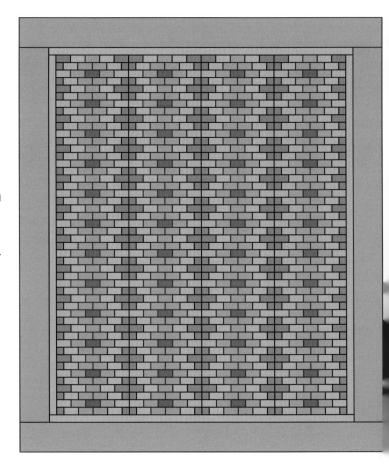

Mosaic uses a rectangular block Using blocks that are not square opens up more design possibilities. The quilt is assembled the same as one using square blocks. After sewing the blocks into vertical rows add a slice of Strip Set 1 to the bottom of each row to balance the pattern.

This design can also be assembled using a horizontal set. Turn the drawing to the right 90° so the pieces run vertically. This makes the design resemble a Grandmothers Flower Garden pattern.

Photo on page 18
10" x 4" block
Vertical Setting

Yardage

		Wall 40" x 42" 24 blocks (3 x 8)	Lap 50" x 58" 48 blocks (4 x 12)	Twin 70" x 100" 100 blocks (5 x 20)	Full 84" x 102" 154 blocks (7 x 22)	Queen 90" x 108" 154 blocks (7 x 22)	King 110" x 116" 216 blocks (9 x 24)
Color "A"		1/8	1/4	1/3	1/2	1/2	3/4
Color "B"		5/8	1-1/8	2-1/4	3-1/4	3-1/4	4-7/8
Color "C"		5/8	1-1/4	2-1/2	3-2/3	3-2/3	5-1/2
Color "D"		1/3	3/4	1-3/8	2	2	3-1/8
Border # 1		1/4	1/4	1/3	3/8	3/8	1/2
Border # 2		5/8	3/4	1	3/4	1-1/4	1-3/8
Border # 3				1-3/8	1-1/4	1-3/4	1-7/8
Binding		1/2	5/8	7/8	1	1	1-1/8
Backing		1-1/3	3-1/8	6	7-5/8	8-1/8	9-7/8

utting

		Wall	Lap	Twin	Full	Queen	King
Color "A" 2-1/2"		1	2	4	6	6	9
Color "B" 2-1/2"		7	14	28	42	42	63
Color "C" 2-1/2"		8	16	32	48	48	72
Color "D" 2-1/2"		2	4	8	12	12	18
1-1/2"		4	8	16	24	24	36
order # 1 1-1/2"		4	5	7	8	8	10
order # 2 4-1/2"		4	5	7		9	10
2-1/2"					9		
order # 3 5-1/2"				8		10	11
4-1/2"					9		
inding 3"		5	6	9	10	10	11

trip Sets

	Wall	Lap	Twin	Full	Queen	King
of strip sets	1	2	4	6	6	9

Row 1

2-1/2" "D"
2-1/2" "C"
2-1/2" "B"
2-1/2" "C"
2-1/2" "D"

Rows 2 & 4

1-1/2" "D"
2-1/2" "C"
2-1/2" "B"
2-1/2" "B"
2-1/2" "C"
1-1/2" "D"

Row 3

2-1/2" "C"
2-1/2" "B"
2-1/2" "A"
2-1/2" "B"
2-1/2" "C"

37

DESIGNING YOUR OWN

This section explains how to calculate yardage and cutting for original designs. The example below is for a 10" block. The process is the same for 12" blocks, just use the 12" charts.

Make several copies of the 10" block, below, and page 39. Notice that the yardage and cutting for the borders, binding, and backing are the same for any quilts made with the same size blocks. You may wish to enlarge the design sheet and block.

Color in a design with colored pencil or pens on the block chart. Next take a design sheet and color in at least four blocks. Keep trying until you have a design that repeats in a pleasing pattern. Assign a fabric letter to each color used.

Each rectangle on the chart equals a 2-1/2" strip of fabric. Each square equals a 1-1/2" strip. Count the rectangles with "A" in them and note this number. Count the squares with "A" in them and write it down. Repeat for each color until all squares and rectangles are counted.

Some designs may have two or more adjacent strips of the same color. I have found that cutting wider strips to replace the adjacent strips causes the eye to focus on that wider strip. Because of this I find that using only 1-1/2" and 2-1/2" strips gives the best results.

The lap size uses one full strip set for each row, so it is easiest to work with. Record the number of 2-1/2" rectangles and 1-1/2" squares for Fabric "A" on the lap size on the cutting chart. Repeat for each fabric. These numbers are the number of strips to cut of each size, from each fabric, for a lap quilt.

Once the lap chart is completed you can calculate the strips for any size quilt. Simply multiply the strips needed by the number of strip sets required (last column on cutting chart) for the quilt you want to make.

Fill out the yardage chart. Use a calculator to make this step easier.

For fabric "A" - Multiply the # of strips by the size

9 strips x 2-1/2" =	22-1/2"
1 strip x 1-1/2" =	1-1/2"
Total	24"
Add 10% (shrinkage, uneven cuts)	2.4"
	26.4"
Round up to a cutable yardage -	27" or 3/4 yard

This is the minimum to buy for this fabric. I buy at least 1/4 yard extra of each. Continue to calculate the yardage for each fabric in your design.

The yardage conversion chart below is helpful. If, for example, you need 92" of one fabric, add 10% or 9.2", to total 101.2". Find the yardage on the chart that is less than 101. In this case it would be 72" or 2 yards. Subtract 72" from 101.2 to get 29.2". Find the yardage on the chart that is closest to the amount needed. In this case it is 31.5" or 7/8 yard. The amount needed of this fabric is 2-7/8 yards.

YARDAGE CONVERSION CHART

1/8 yd. = 4.5"
1/4 yd. = 9"
1/3 yd. = 12"
3/8 yd. = 13.5"
1/2 yd. = 18"
5/8 yd. = 22.5"
2/3 yd. = 24"
3/4 yd. = 27"
7/8 yd. = 31.5"
1 yd. = 36"
2 yds. = 72"
3 yds. = 108"
4 yds. = 144"
5 yds. = 180"
6 yds. = 216"
7 yds. = 252"
8 yds. = 288"

10" block

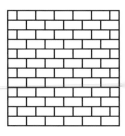

12" block

Yardage - 10" blocks

	Wall 40" x 40" 9 blocks (3 x 3)	Lap 50" x 60" 20 blocks (4 x 5)	Twin 70" x 100" 40 blocks (5 x 8)	Full 84" x 104" 63 blocks (7 x 9)	Queen 90" x 110" 63 blocks (7 x 9)	King 110" x 110" 81 blocks (9 x 9)
Color "A"						
Color "B"						
Color "C"						
Color "D"						
Color "E"						
Color "F"						
Border # 1	1/4	1/4	1/3	3/8	3/8	1/2
Border # 2	5/8	3/4	1	3/4	1-1/4	1-3/8
Border # 3			1-3/8	1-1/4	1-3/4	1-7/8
Binding	3/8	5/8	7/8	1	1	1-1/8
Backing	1-1/4	3-1/8	6	7-5/8	8	9-7/8

Cutting - 10" blocks

	Wall	Lap	Twin	Full	Queen	King
Color "A"						
2-1/2"						
1-1/2"						
Color "B"						
2-1/2"						
1-1/2"						
Color "C"						
2-1/2"						
1-1/2"						
Color "D"						
2-1/2"						
1-1/2"						
Color "E"						
2-1/2"						
1-1/2"						
Border # 1						
1-1/2"	4	5	7	8	8	9
Border # 2						
4-1/2"	4	5	7		9	10
2-1/2"				9		
Border # 3						
5-1/2"			8		10	11
4-1/2"				9		
Binding						
3"	4	6	9	10	10	11
of strip sets	1/2	1	2	3	3	3-1/2

Design sheet

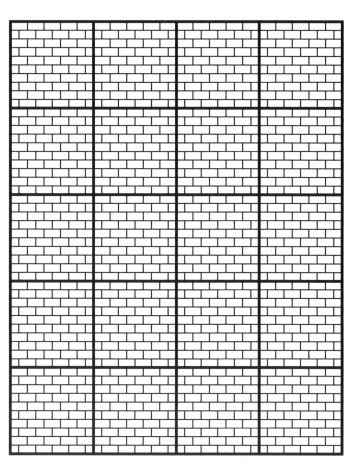

Yardage - 12" blocks

	Wall 34" x 34" 4 blocks (2 x 2)	Lap 58" x 70" 20 blocks (4 x 5)	Twin 70" x 106" 40 blocks (5 x 8)	Full 84" x 108" 48 blocks (6 x 8)	Queen 92" x 116" 48 blocks (6 x 8)	King 108" x 108" 64 blocks (8 x 8)
Color "A"						
Color "B"						
Color "C"						
Color "D"						
Color "E"						
Color "F"						
Border # 1	1/4	1/3	3/8	1/2	1/2	1/2
Border # 2	5/8	7/8	1-1/4	3/4	1-1/4	7/8
Border # 3				1	1-3/4	1-1/4
Binding	3/8	2/3	7/8	1	1-1/8	1-1/8
Backing	1-1/8	3-5/8	6-1/3	7-5/8	8-1/3	9-5/8

Cutting - 12" blocks

Design sheet

	Wall	Lap	Twin	Full	Queen	King
Color "A"						
2-1/2"						
1-1/2"						
Color "B"						
2-1/2"						
1-1/2"						
Color "C"						
2-1/2"						
1-1/2"						
Color "D"						
2-1/2"						
1-1/2"						
Color "E"						
2-1/2"						
1-1/2"						
Border # 1						
1-1/2"	4	6	8	9	9	10
Border # 2						
4-1/2"	4	6	9		9	
2-1/2"				9		10
Border # 3						
5-1/2"					10	
3-1/2"				9		11
Binding						
3"	4	7	9	10	11	11
# of strip sets	1/4	1	2	2	2	3

40